Homefront

Homefront

Poems by Patricia Monaghan

WordTech Editions

Published by WordTech Editions
P.O. Box 541106
Cincinnati, OH 45254-1106

Typeset in Iowan Old Style and Gill Sans by WordTech
Communications LLC, Cincinnati, OH

ISBN: 1933456094
LCCN: 2005933900

Poetry Editor: Kevin Walzer
Business Editor: Lori Jareo

Visit us on the web at www.wordtechweb.com

Cover photograph: clipart.com, used with permission

Acknowledgements

The following poems have been previously published in anthologies:

Call it Courage: Women Transcending Violence. "Home Movies."
  Miriam Harris, editor. Temple University Press,
  1993.
Fresh Water: Poems from the Rivers, Lakes and Streams. "The
  River, Built by Saddam Hussein and Named the
  Mother of Battles, Speaks." Jennifer Bosveld, editor.
  Pudding House Press, 2002.
From the Listening Place: Languages of Intuition. "Hmong Pa-
  ndau, Embroideries of the Laos Hills," "The River,
  Constructed by Saddam Hussein and Named the
  Mother of Battles, Speaks." "At Quartz Creek, At
  Fifteen." Margaret Blanchard, editor. Astarte Shell
  Press, 1997.
Irish-American Poetry. "Kevin Barry Gave His Young Life."
  Dan Tobin, editor. Notre Dame University Press.
  2005.
Poets against the War. "The Woman of Baghdad." Sam
  Hamill, editor. The Nation Books, 2003.
Prayers to Protest: Poems that Center and Bless Us. "The Tiniest
  of Prayers." Jennifer Bosveld, editor. Pudding House
  Publications, 1998.
The Hermit Kingdom: Poems of the Korean War. "Home
  Movies," "Dream Details," "Accidents and Loss and
  War." "Now, In His Age, the Inner Sea." Paul M.
  Edwards, editor. Center for the Study of the Korean
  War, 1995.
*Writing our Way Out of the Dark: An Anthology by Child Abuse
  Survivors.* "Knowing the Bomb So Well." Elizabeth
  Claman, editor. Queen of Swords Press, 1995.

The following poems have been previously published in journals:

Black Bear Review. "Home Movies," "A Reply to the German Man on Homer Spit who Believes War to be Inevitable."

Caprice. "Here Be Dragons," "Accidents and Loss and War," "Isaac Afterwards."

Event. "Quartz Creek at Fifteen."

Long Shot. "The Peace Conference Shares Space with the Arms Bazaar."

Out of Line: Writings on Peace and Justice. "Geography Lessons," "Knowing the Bomb so Well."

Permafrost. "Hmong Pa-ndau, Embroideries of the Laos Hills."

Poetry Motel. "Mars in the Northern Sky."

River Oak Review. "Here Be Dragons," "Knowing the Bomb So Well," "Doll Crematorium."

Sing Heavenly Muse! "In County Mayo."

Sou'wester. "Kevin Barry Gave His Young Life."

Women and Language. "Geography Lessons," "Friendly Fire," "Patriot Game."

Selections of poems were previously published in the following chapbooks:

Homefront (Foothills Press Poets on Peace Series, 2003)
Soldier's Heart (Chanting Press, 2004)

Contents

Collateral Damage

In memoriam,
Lt. Col. E. J. Monaghan (USAF, Ret)

My childhood.
    Sitting on his knee.
    Telling him my hurts.
    His arms around me.

My girlhood.
    Playing games with him.
    Reading to each other.
    His shoulder to rest on.

My youth.
    Learning what he knew.
    Showing off my gifts.
    His eyes shining with pride.

My life.
    None of this happened.
    It was taken from us.
    This is what war does.

PART ONE

Home Movies, 1954

A Japanese meal has been made,
and sake warmed and sipped, and
the girls dressed up in small kimonos.

The conversation has been
instructive, for the children,
and slightly bawdy, for the rest.

At least one mention has been made
of Panmunjong. There has been
a bilingual dirty song or two.

The daughters now bring out
the wood dolls from Japan and show
how the elaborately dressed hair

can be removed, leaving the head
momentarily bald while another
wig is brought from the case.

As the children grow sleepy
a sheet is tacked against the wall
and the projector taken out.

There is a little game to play
with sake cups, so that
everyone is drunk by the time

the movies begin. Aerial views
of Korean fields, paddies, blue
distant hills. Smoke and flame,

real war movies. The men drink
and retell the squadron jokes
while the women clear and clean.

The children, holding their dolls,
watch the silent bombs land
on the bed sheet, over and over.

Knowing the Bomb So Well

After the nightly news and four martinis
he quietly begins to draw the inner workings

of the bomb, knowing the explosion needed
to ignite fission does not itself comprise

the real event; how compartmentalized the bomb,
of necessity, is, to keep the elements

separate until it impacts on target;
with what care the bomb is timed so that

from the moment of release it proceeds
inexorably to detonation.

It is necessary then to explain his drawing
in detail to the children, before they go to bed.

After a few moments he quizzes them:
What are the proper names of the bombs dropped

on Nagasaki, Hiroshima? Who captained
the Enola Gay? How does a prisoner

of war answer the enemy? The children
do not speak. They know release has occurred,

the elements are colliding, impact is inevitable.
It is always a first-strike situation. Always.

Dream Details

She is a child hiding in bamboo,
She does not recognize the soldiers
coming after her, it does not matter

that she knows nothing, she has
never known anything, she sees red fire,
the next time they are above her,

she is running across a field, a tiny
moving target, red on green, she hears
a long whine, over and over she dreams

footprints on her face, floral tattoos,
while across the hall her father
sleeps, groaning with, growing into

the same dreams, same dreams,
the ambush, the betrayal, aerial
surveillance, interrogation, and wakes

with no memory, cannot recall any wound
a Korean girl wore like a blood tattoo,
any child running across bamboo fields alone.

Shelter

Her bed is built of eighteen
cartons of c-rations. The bookcase:
cartons with wood shelves.

Water jugs line

the closet. The dresser is stuffed
with iodine pills and bandages
and rounds of ammo.

But no guns.

The guns are upstairs, because
there will be time, when the war
begins, to grab them from

walls and closets,

time while the family gathers
in the safety of the shelter.
Time to load the guns

against the neighbors

who will be banging
and pleading at the locked door.
Until the war starts, this

is her room.

Hers to decorate. She hides
the cartons under a red damask
fringed cloth from Japan,

from the war,

and beneath a blue coverlet,
too big for the bed, hanging to the floor.
You can hardly see the bullets stacked

beneath the dolls.

Geographies

children of mountains
learn
to read the looming peaks,
learn how
coming weather writes itself
on changeful
faces, learn to recognize
the way to secret
valleys
where they can be
safe
from storms that
lash
whatever is left
open and exposed—

they hate the plains, those foreign unpredictable lands
where everything comes sudden and extreme and wild,
where they never know where to hide when storms come
down,
where the land seems intent upon lulling them into a state
of bored inattention that can only bring them harm—

children
of mountains
read
each day's storms and promises
with great care
and
great attention
and
without knowing
there are

different kinds
of
land,
of
weather—

Loaded

They were always taught that all guns were loaded.
It was a way, he said, to keep them safe.
Don't you notice, he said, how people get shot
by pistols they think are unloaded? The gun
on the living room shelf, the unhidden
Lugar, the rack full of rifles: the children

knew each one was death. Now children,
he'd ask, his hand on a gun, is this loaded?
Mute chorus of yes. Mute yearning to hide.
That was their home. At school they were safe
even when textbooks talked about guns
and described how the buffalo hunters would shoot

and buffalo crumple down dead, one shot
enough to bring down the biggest. No child
in that school had ever seen bison, gunned
down or living, seen meat being loaded
on travois by leather-clad scouts, safety
bolts on their guns; no child had worn hides

or rode on the plains. But in history hid
critical truths that they sought about shooting
and fear and escape. Learn and be safe,
history whispered its promise to children
like them, learn and be safe. But a loaded
gun holds only one promise. A gun,

any gun, threatens use of a gun
no matter how they tried to hide
in books, no matter how they loaded
themselves down with schoolwork. A shot

or two in the evening, then, children,
he'd say, don't think the world's safe,

then he'd tell how once he had saved
someone's life with that very gun
over there on the wall and then children,
he'd say, be prepared for the worst, never hide
from attackers, they all deserve shooting,
so all guns must always be loaded.

Even dreams weren't safe, for hiding
in them were guns, aimed, ready to shoot.
Even children know this: loading leads to unloading.

Kevin Barry Gave His Young Life

In the grandmother's front closet,
packed away among the winter coats,

was a picture of him, hanging from
the gallows tree, somewhere in Ireland,

sometime in the past, during one
of the revolutions they sang about

at the picnics and the parties. Kevin
Barry gave his young life for the cause

of liberty, and wasn't his execution
at Tuam, near Grandpa's Mayo home,

or was that Roddy McCorley, who went
to die on the bridge that day, not Kevin

hanging there, another martyr
for the cause, in the front closet. Grandpa

knew all the songs, and the uncles did
too, and they drank to old Ireland and

to Father Murphy from old Kilcormick
who spurred up the rocks with a warning

cry, and Kelly the Boy from Killane, and
Dauntless Red Hugh, and Connaught and

Gallowglasses thronged from the mountain
passes and quietly, so quietly, Kevin Barry

hung there in the front closet, just
exactly the size of a standing child,

a child who might open the closet
to get a winter coat and see—his eyes

bulging, his head skewed painfully
to the side—how painful rebellion

was, how hopeless, how useless,
while in the kitchen the uncles

sang rebel liturgies, sang and drank
in the long evenings, and nobody

ever knew the way the children
pushed each other into the closet

yelling, Kevin Barry, Kevin Barry,
while the trapped child screamed.

Minstrel Boy

She loved songs about young men
dying for freedom, heroes all, but
she loved "The Minstrel Boy" best.
She imagined wiping his face

as he lay dying, his tender eyes
gazing into hers, an instant
of recognition. She was like him
in so many ways: small and

fierce and proud. He saw that.
And so he gave his harp to her,
no need to savage it, no need
to stop its melodies. Weeping,

heart pounding, full of purpose,
she stood tall and carried on,
playing his wild harp's battle song
while he joined the ghost parade.

She could see them, all the dead boys
marching together in perfect time,
uniforms clean and pressed and smart,
faces serious but bright with pride,

she could see them, all the soldiers
dead for all the causes, and she loved
that vision of their neat parade
from battlefield up to heaven,

for surely soldiers went to heaven
when they died, surely soldiers
did no wrong but were only hurt
like children by those with bigger guns.

She loved young men in songs who
died for their causes, heroes all.
There was something so noble about them.
Something so innocent and pure.

Sunday Afternoon at the Officers' Club

She was wearing her blue dress
with the design like water that day.

There were movies for the kids
so that the parents could drink

away the afternoon undisturbed.
The bar was loud and smoky.

She stood silent at the door to
the bar, looking in. She wanted to

go home. She had left the dark
room downstairs where on the screen

a train was perpetually rolling
over western hills, with shooting

coming always from above,
always from above the train,

and the sharpshooters were
killing the passengers, and her

dreams were like that, her dreams
always had danger coming from

above while she ran fast and
helpless through the fields.

The bar was smoky and loud.
Her father was singing.

Her mother was wearing that red dress. She did not go in.

On Cheyenne Mountain

There was a pagoda-like building near a rocky
overlook and, nearby, a little mountain zoo

that was their destination one Sunday afternoon.
They drove down from the base to the north.

The soldier told the children that the mountain
was the petrified remains of a dinosaur.

As they drove closer, the children could see
the rocky spikes of the dragon's back,

the long thin tail, the rounded bulk
of the stony head. They were frightened

even though they knew the dinosaur
was dead and could not harm them.

There were bears in the zoo, and other animals
live and dangerous in the thin mountain air.

There was a long steep drop from the pagoda
over the rocks along the mountainside.

After the long ascent came the long descent
when the father told them something else:

that the mountain was hollow, that it was
filled with machines to win all wars,

that he would be there when the war
began, he would be safe from missiles—

the ICBM's roaring from the red west—and
he would fight back, fight back and win.

There was no room for the children
in the mountain. There was no room

for the mother. There was no room
for the dog. The children were silent

as they drove north again. The children
looked out the back window at the dinosaur.

Accidents and Loss and War

The son begged for a dog, so it was he
who had to feed it and walk it and,
when it was killed, bury it. He disappeared
into the woods near the duck pond.
It was spring, the ground was hard,
the grave took hours. When he came back,
it was over. He never mentioned it again.

The next year, his best friend's gun
discharged during cleaning; they ruled out
suicide—he was an officer's son, daily
communicant, although why he was pointing
a loaded gun at his head was anybody's guess—and
the son locked himself in his room for three
days after the funeral, and never mentioned it again.

Later, when he joined the service, he liked
to say there were no accidents, everything
was chosen, every man was clear about everything
he did, plane crashes were deliberate, war was part
of the pattern, the brave always survived.
On the ruins of love he built a theory:
they had chosen to die. He'd decided to live.

White Glove Inspection

The father was commanding officer,
the oldest son was NCO. Because mother

and the baby were away, it was father's duty
to maintain order. So every morning

he marched through every room, testing
every surface with a clean white glove.

The boy marched somberly behind the father,
stood at attention at each door while inspection

took place. The girl stood rigid at the foot
of the bed, saluting the inspection team.

She was never good enough. He always
found the pale streak of dust on the vanity,

the dust-tangled sock at the back of the closet,
the paper doll stuck in the tight-sheeted bed.

And there was always punishment, sharp
and quickly administered, a ruler on the palm.

This was the way she learned to be still.
To hate those in power. To hate as a way

to protect disorder and wild joy.
But to hide and be small and be still.

Doll Crematorium

One ordinary Saturday
a drunken soldier burns
all his daughter's dolls
out behind the house in
a cement incinerator normally
used for household refuse.

The way he sees it, it is
time. Enough of the mess,
the chaos. Ten years
is long enough for childhood.
Time to enforce some reason.
Time to get things in control.

In her eyes, it is
murder—the paper dolls like
tinder, the Japanese dolls
curling into smoke against
the mountains, the long-legged
dolls melting like flesh—

and if later she misses the broken
dolls most, it is because she
was the one who'd wounded
them, and she knew how and she
knew why. Broken dolls hold
only history, no surprises.

She'd thought them invulnerable
in their fractured grace; the doll
hospital could not restore their first
integrity; the damage had been done.
She had found comfort in that.
She had never thought of this.

Munchkins in War, 1962

Choices were simple in those days.
Everyone wanted to be Glinda,
the Good Witch, no one wanted

to be the Wicked Witch of the West.
Girls like me, who failed to be clearly
either, got to be munchkins, got to skip

down the painted paper road singing
follow-follow-follow-follow, got to rehearse
for relentless hours after school, off base.

I cannot remember what we wore, how
we fixed our hair, who held my hand
as we skipped down the yellow paper road—

I remember October darkness after dress
rehearsal, five or six military brats coming
home, singing loudly in a crowded car,

reaching the locked gates still singing
follow-follow-follow-follow, I remember
men with guns surrounding the car,

I remember October, I remember Cuba—
someplace far to the east, like Glinda—
I remember rolling down my window

to tell the men not to worry, we were
only little munchkins, nothing wicked—
I remember the gun. The gun in my face.

A young man's frozen eyes in a frozen
face. I remember the gun being cocked.
I remember a trigger finger, twitching.

After that, I knew it would not be easy
to tell good from wickedness. After that,
I knew being small offered no protection.

PART TWO

Songs of the Kerry Madwoman

1. Keening

women shawled in black
blacken the air with cries,
crying over torn bodies,
bodying forth sorrow,
sorrowing for sons, fathers,
son's fathers, tearing
tears from torn hearts,

while I who cannot remember keenly
cannot keen what I cannot remember

2. Before

On morning-shrouded mountains
birds cry out as day begins.
Goats clatter as they graze
shrouded from sight in the haze.

Morning mist is an wide door
to the forgotten. Before,
before, before. Memory
mists my eyes. I become sea

suddenly, salt and surging,
weedy and wanton, urgent
to tumble forth treasures, storm
fragments, salty shards, warnings

in detritus of the drowned,
warnings of what might be found.
I would linger longer here
half-drowned, half-disappeared,

but the bright mist burns away
in the strong sun of the day
and the sea in me subsides
as I scale the mountainsides.

3. Rainpool

Who waits within small water? Who watches so warily?
Fur-covered fugitive, wolf-woman who terrifies travelers. It
is I, mad mountainy Mis, left alone, learning to be loathly.
Look: mad Mis, tear-torn, touches trembling water.

4. Freedom

mountain morning:
blue breeze blowing,
singing soft summons
to taste thin time

before breath breaks
off—oh
wandering wild
on open ordinary
earth, everything

alive, all ablaze
with wondrous warmth—
mad maiden Mis
draws down dawn

5. Stranger

who strides towards me in the sunlight
like the dream of a lost dream
who stands so deep in the shadow
but green as a ripe sloe gleams

who watches the weather gather
above gray seas in the south
who waits like a weary hunter
but smiles with a tender mouth

who hunts me here on my mountain
who makes a song of the sky
who comes to my cave of silence
with a strong and violent cry

who draws my dreams together
and tethers them in his heart
who ruins me with remembrance
who hunts an embrace with such art

6. Music

The air grows sweet with memory:
somewhere in the dim distance
someone plays a melody
that rouses visions. Instants

of pleasure, pure, unshadowed.
But some sorrow hides within:
Was there not some episode
that sang so sadly? Again,

again, that faint remembrance.
Again, again, that moment
dim and distant. Violence
there, and bloodshed, some event

that transformed me utterly
and drove me to this mountain.
Who now comes to tenderly
sing away my dark fur skin?

Who comes to take wilderness
from my soul? Can he perceive
the girl beneath this beastliness?
And will he hold me as I grieve?

7. Father

Suddenly I see:
sea suddenly blood,
blood-tossed tide,
tidings of dread,
of the dead, the dear earth
unearthing uncountable ravening
ravens to eat eyes—
I see swords strike,
stricken men made
mad, even the sweet sun
sundered from her sky—

Sky and sand and war.
Warriors dying. One,
one man, means most.
Mostly forgotten, mad
maiden Mis gone wild
in wilderness. Forgetting
forgotten now. Father,
father, my dear blood,
bloodied, battered. Dead.

Dead. No. Not dead.
Dear one, no, no.
Not dead. I read
red poems pouring forth,
poring for meaning,
me and you, your blood,
blood in my hands,
hands full of blood in my mouth,
mouthing your name, no,
not dead, no, drinking,

drinking my doom—
my doomed darling—
daring to drink your blood.

8. Murderer

Fionn found father
in bloody battle.
Swords sang sharp
dirges of death.

I watched well-matched
wanton warriors
fighting fiercely,
daring death.

I saw sword slash
hard, the heart,
father falling,
damp with death.

I ran to raise
his heavy head,
hold his hand,
delay his death.

A gasp. And gone.
Slaughtered. Slain.
Was I more mad
to drink his death?

9. Rage

Heave, heavens, pound down, drown
and lightning-smite all kin-killers.
Open, earth, eat each hellbound
brute butcher, bruise him, bury him.
Roar, rock, thunder through ground
grown rank from his hard hazard.
Bay, bark, bellow, beasts, surround
him, hem him in, hunt him, haunt him.
Surge, sea, deafen the death-dealer, sound
dread depths, flood forth, finish him.

10. Rain

What falls, falls, falls? What wets my fur-face? Why spend small water? What solace? Water will never nurture him, not him. Not him. Rain, rivers, streams, seas, water falls. Falls, falls, falls. Mad Mis melting. Wet with sorrow. What solace. What solace.

11. You

Oh, I know you now, sweet harper,
from happy times in the halls
of my lost father. I forgot
how your music moves. Not all

men move me so, not all music
moves wilderness within me.
Come here closer, handsome harper.
Make music on me, set free

the songs that stopped so long ago.
Let me music you as well.
Music is not far from madness
and I, Mis, know madness well.

When reason ran, I ran after:
wrathful, wounded, weeping, wild.
Touch me and you touch my history:
crazed woman, enemy, child.

Hold me, harp me, strum me, stroke me
until wildness wings through me.
Sea me, shore me, coast me, cloud me,
until music mists through me.

12. Poet

I drank deep. Warm, when bloodied body fell. What more wild-making? Filling my mouth. Blood into blood. What more maddening? Mis on mountain, loathly, loveless. Where went music? I drank deep, blood into blood.

I drink deep. Lust, love, longing: wildness into wildness. Desire deter death? Never. Death deter desire? Never. Not if mountains melt, not if seas smoke. Drink death; drink desire.

Wildness into wildness, I drink deep.

PART THREE

At the Pow-Wow

My friend asks,
why are you not dancing?

In eagle feathers, bearing pipes,
sons and fathers circle.

They call for warrior
families to dance.

Korea, Vietnam, Desert
Storm: they name the names.

My friend asks,
why are you not dancing?

Daughters circle light as deer.
Mothers circle, grave and stately.

They call for warrior
families to dance.

They call on me to dance.
I do not move.

My friend asks,
why are you not dancing?

My father's upraised hand.
The tattoo pattern of my bruises.

They call for warrior
families to dance.

My heart sour with old anger.
My heart stiff with old pain.

My warrior father knows
why I am not dancing.

Isaac Afterwards

Your face did not change
at all. The lines were there

from the start, the ones
that fell into that singular

expression of delighted servility.
I had never noticed it, playing

near you in the evening light.
Yet after that moment, when

I looked up at your raised
hand and saw your face suffused

with longing—the longing to be
a son again, not the father of sons,

to be commanded, to be enslaved,
yes, when I saw your thankfulness

that there were orders to follow,
that responsibility lay elsewhere—

after that, when you raised
your hand in greeting, when you

raised your hand in prayer,
it was all the same to me,

your child whom you spared
only because you follow orders.

Temporary Duty

Midnight in the house near the runway.

The engine noise awakens me:
jets whining off to guard the DEW line.

Their wing lights strafe the window.

Sudden sharpness of urine:
my sister panics, does not wake.

One more time, I begin to die.

It has something to do with stopping
the heart, I know. It is done

through will: death as proof of strength.

I read somewhere of the possibility
of drawing the soul up through the body

and out the head. It starts with the toes

which grow cold under the blanket. I can
manage that part. But then my will fails.

An hour passes. My heart is loud as a jet.

Only my toes are cold. I despise myself:
my body's compromises, its hot rebellion,

its refusal to follow orders.

The Patriot Game

All our songs were one song:
invasion, resistance, betrayal,

then martyrdom for the cause.
At ten I knew the words

"quisling" and "Hessian,"
"Gallowglasses," "Fenian"

and knew that history meant
rising and rebellion and defeat.

Our heritage was full of martial
cadences and sentimental words

and all our songs were one song:
young men dying for Ireland.

There were no songs for men
made mad by war, no songs

for those who drank to still
the bloody nightmares, no songs

for children, mothers, wives,
no music and no words

for all the ruined ones.
Heroes die. They have it easy.

In County Mayo

The turf settles as we again assign
blame for the unfathomable, cousins
in a house perishing with loss: sons
prisoned or dead, the border at hand,
a war at table, wounded mother, father
bitter with clarity. My left leg
scalds from the blaze, my right
is numb from a doorway breeze.

It is one a.m. Hot and damp in a crowded
bedroom, someone coughs and calls from
another bed. Over here, secret forces
evade the grip of security police;
there is a plot to overthrow
the government and counter attempts
to unmask sixteen conspirators.

The dreams are familiar as cousins
and jump-rope rhymes, even the fear
in them, even the decisions.
It was too easy when I said
there were things I might die for
but I didn't know if I could kill.
The dreams, the dreams. This split
island and its wars, grandfather
songs, glory-o, glory-o, insurgent
histories, legacy of night.

Mozart on Parnell Square

It is easy to hate what is ugly and cruel.
The gun at the hip, the gas cloud of doom,
the rape of a child—it is easy to hate
a world that allows them. But here in this room

full of beautiful strangers who sit among paintings
and flowers, the music forgets all that pain.
The flute flits among us, the viola dances,
and we're washed of our fears by a musical rain.

It lasts only an hour. Outside, the world thunders again.
A young woman begs on the bridge. A hapless old man
mutters drunkenly by, and hopeless young men yell a curse.
An old woman cries. These were the sounds we ran

from when we entered the room. These are the sounds
the music avoids and allows, the music can never displace.
It is easy to hate what is ugly and cruel.
But this terrible pureness—this shadowless space—

To the Rebels in My Dreams

You were always running, trying to place
phone calls to missing members or, in the worst
cases, to the authorities. When you were caught
in public with your coded messages, you claimed
you found them in vending machines, you claimed
no knowledge of revolt, you claimed and claimed
until you killed yourself or turned traitor.

Once I remember the police bursting
into a castellated hideout, all of them armed
with glistening iron, all of you nailing
yourselves to the walls with suicide arrows.
After that, disguised as a mime troupe,
you entertained at fairs and rituals, but
the glances exchanged among you made it clear
the plots went on, the reasons for rebellion
had become traditional, skits and ballads now,
certain habits of clothing and tattooing.
You even talked to me once, on the sidewalk,
in undisguised terms of the significance
of whiteface, but then blindfolded me and
held me captive at the spider-temple while you
discussed assassination as a theatrical device.

Now you appear in leather and bikers' helmets
and bulldoze my forest to landscape a lawn
with Louis Quatorze filigrees of snapdragons
and azaleas, and I of course recognize you,

and know that next you will return disguised
as unemployed farmers protesting flowerbeds
where crops could grow and placing scarecrows

oddly along the rows, and that crows will then
roost there in despite, and that the crows will
be yet another disguise, one with wings, for you.

Friendly Fire

Years later, I tried to talk to him about Kent State,
how I had heard the news at a campus rally,
how the newsreels—faces of students, guardsmen,

so young and so familiar—haunted me. How
I could have been one of them. How my brother
could have been on the other side, shooting.

I imagined this might shatter the silence
between us. Silence I had preferred to
"I'll give you the back of my hand for that"

and "you're asking for it now." Noisy silence,
silence filled with aimlessness and evasion.
Silence in which estrangement roared.

He listened stolidly. His voice was calm
and precise. "They were traitors," he said.
"Traitors should be shot. If I were there,"

he said, "and you on the other side," he said,
"committing treason, I'd have no choice but shoot.
Keep this up, I might have to shoot you now."

Jeptha's Daughter Laments

My face against the nettle
My face against the gravel
My face against the thorn

My hands filled with rushes
My hands filled with briars
My hands filled with my hair

This is my body you seeded
This is my body you fed
This is my body you sacrifice

There was a promise you made
There was a promise you made
There was a promise you made

Before the pledge to your lord
Before the pact with your god
Before the deal for your fate

In a moment of pleasure
In a moment of loss
In a moment near death

You gave a wordless cry
You gave a gasp of grief
You gave a spasm of life

I was that promise
I am that promise
You are breaking your promise

You are breaking your promise
Father, father, father
You have broken my heart

After the Attack

Some vitamins, I said, are known
to heal scars, even on the heart.

But the scars, he said, aren't bad,
They're strong, knots in the muscle.

You could take it anyway, I said,
who knows? It can't hurt.

No, he said, the scars bind up
the heart and make it stronger.

I take vitamins, I said, I wonder
if I'm weakening my heart.

No, he said, you have no scars,
so take them if you want to.

How can you say my heart isn't
scarred, I said, you know it is.

That fever when you were little?
he said. That what you mean?

Yes, I said, fevers, murmurs,
you know all about the damage.

Oh well, he said, you've taken
the stuff, it's too late now.

Now, in His Age, the Inner Sea

He drives up a narrow road along a cliff
above the sea, somehow he recognizes it,
this sea, somehow he knows this road, but

in Korea he would not be driving; he would
fly; he'd never see the place from such
an ordinary angle; he would never be exposed

this way: bullets, bombs, rockets, all
at once explode beside him, behind him,
up ahead, force him off the road—into the sea—

The truck is flying, flying, the air lit up
with fire all around, the sea opening a sudden
almond eye beneath him, he is flying

into the eye, he is being devoured by the sea—but
he was never on that road, he was in a different
danger, the choppy prop-sound, the round sound

of the brown earth cratering beneath his bombs,
the splatter sound of strafing and the ripping,
the shredding sound of aircraft fabric—no—

The truck falls from the cliff.
A blue splash: the man drowning.
He tries to float; he tries to swim.

His efforts sap his strength. The sea swells.
It holds up and pulls down, both at once.
A huge wave aims the man towards shore.

At Quartz Creek

I climbed a knotty cottonwood and
carved my name; I have a short name;
it did not take long; but while I did
my brother, racing a boat around the lake,
fell in. While I was in the tree the boat
was lost, my brother saved, my father furious—

but there, surrounded by tree fleece and unaware
of any other threat of loss, I had slipped away
like the boat from my brother's control, had
felt myself slowly sinking under life,
had cried as I carved, wondering

would I remember my name blazoned
on a tree at Kenai Lake—sure I would
forget—crying for all I knew I had already
forgotten, all those times I knew myself

for just the time it takes to climb a tree
or uproot a wild onion or find the first
spring patches of asparagus, those moments
of myself, and I was certain I would forget
this one, I was certain this would be
the last, that I would soon forget
myself and die.

I fled into my tent and cried into my old brown
sleeping bag till dinner, when I sat pensive
and silent, trying to keep hold of that moment
while my father scolded and the babies screamed.

I have come to that lake for the first time since,
boats roar across its greenness and I do not even

search for that tree—in twenty years it will have
fallen—but the cottonwoods give me back that memory,
I send back to that girl some consolation—
my remembering her, my still remaining her—

my spirit touches hers, my own, and she
quiets, sitting at that redwood table,

she stares into the lake, she does not know
it is herself who comforts her, she will not
for many years know that.

Last Run

in the shelter of the bank
torn-fleshed kings

are shadows

beneath stony rapids
too shallow now

to cross

a few hours, a rising tide
and they will be home

for good

nearby my father drifts
in the shadow of a stroke

waiting for

that final tide to rise and
launch him into his last

fierce run

Dancing for My Father

The people wear
their mothers' crests

outlined in buttons
on their blankets

The peoples' songs
follow motherlines

The people dance
for their mothers

Except when
the drum changes

and they dance
for their fathers

Today of
all days when

my father lies
near death,

they invite strangers
into the dance

for the fathers
and I stand

in their midst
dancing for him

singing with them,
his child, I

am dancing, dancing,
his child I

am, dancing, becoming
his child dancing

becoming the child
of that father

at last, dancing
for my father

PART FOUR

Soldier's Heart: The Song of Sweeney

1. Din of Battle

They call me madman of the trees, king gone astray, witless
one, mimic of birds, folly's friend. La-la-lee. La-la-loo.
The wild mad king.

Sweeney? I am not Sweeney. Sweeney was a tall strong man
who raised his voice and his arms against anyone who
slighted him.

He was a king, that tall man. A king by birth and battle. I
knew him in his youth. A frenzied man, that Sweeney,
like every man who knows the secret of war. I learned
that secret from him, in my youth.

Lean forward: let me tell you. Let me murmur to you what I
cannot speak into the night's wide listening ear. Let me
tell you of the way, in slant evening light, wine shines
like fresh blood. The way, in mead-tinged candlelight,
the gold hair of a woman glints like weapons clashing.

The way everything grows wild and fierce and vivid, the
night before battle. The blood pricking. The loins
surging. The breath intoxicating. The stars multiplying.

And then the dawn of battle, when nothing is more
beautiful than the enemy, shining with sweat, wanton
with weapons. Everything gleaming bronze. Swords,
helmets, shields, small sharp daggers, gleaming.

Dazzled with the enemy, Sweeney stood on the hillside,
every line of every warrior's face carved into his
memory. Sweeney knew them in that instant. Knew
their hardness. Felt them give way to his greater
hardness.

Legs pounding, arms flailing, lungs bursting. Red. Red.
Screams like frenzied birds. Red. Sweeney drinking
blood from hacked limbs. Red and sweet. I knew that
Sweeney, in my youth. Before Mag Rath. La-la-loo.

Before that battle, when the sound of death filled his ears,
la-la-lee. I wonder where he went, that Sweeney. The
tall strong king. After Mag Rath.
Sweeney was a leader of men. I am a madman of the hills.
Sweeney slept in the bed of a queen. I sleep in treetops,
surrounded by grackles and crows.

2. Before Mag Rath

In the bloody sunset, I saw her.

We were camped beside Mag Rath, the fort-ringed plain. We knew, our foes knew, that at dawn we would hurl ourselves into each others' screaming arms. We were stiff with eagerness.

And then she came.

In the bronze evening, a crow flew from the west. Then another.

Another. Beside small fires, warriors turned red faces to the sun. The flock was a black river in flood. Each crow screaming like a dying man.

It flowed down the center of the plain, that black river. Then a pool opened in the center. We saw a hawk flying amid the crows. A man cheered at the happy omen, a small sound against the river's roar.

Then turbulence. The pool closing around the hawk. Eddies appearing, water splashing over granite. Then, from that river in the sky, a hawk dropping like a rock to earth.

Three times this happened. Three pools, three hawks, three deaths.

The men turned away. All men before battle seek omens. All men before war are druids, full of subtle knowledge. This was no omen they wished to see, no omen they wished to remember.

I did not turn away. The hawks, I saw, were our enemies and we the crows of battle, rending them. That was the way I thought then, when I was Sweeney the king. I thought the future was mine to grasp like the hilt of a sword.

And so I stood by the side of the fort-ringed plain and watched the black river slow to a trickle. A final bird flew forth from the west, the last drop in the river of death. It stopped where three hawks lay like boulders in the center of dawn's battlefield.

The crow circled, circled, circled. Then it dove.

As it reached the ground, the bird changed, in the red light, into a vast woman. A simple-looking one, of the kind who follow armies to cook and clean. A dull hag, but huge, head like a boulder, feet like rocks.

She reached for a hawk. As her hand closed on it, it whitened. She lifted it up, no bird but a white garment that sunset streaked red. She opened a bag at her thick waist and pushed the bloody rag inside.

She picked up each hawk, each bloody rag. She lifted her arms and rose into the air. She flew into the dark eastern sky.

Exultation filled me. How we would destroy them, the enemy. How we would tear their bodies. How we would pierce their hearts. It would be my greatest battle. I did not sleep, waiting for dawn's red signal to raise my sword over the field of Mag Rath.

3. Into the Sky

Battle sounds inside the body. Heavy pounding of metal on
  metal, sword on sword, shield against shield. The
  driving drums, the piercing pipes. Screams of the dying.
At Mag Rath, that bitter music inside me like blood. No
  difference between me and the air I sliced with my
  sword, between me and the men I sliced with my sword.
  I became the stormy music of war.
I was on a small hill in the center of the storm. Men fell
  around me like rain. I heard something like thunder. I
  looked up.
Five boulders flew out of the sky at me. Not boulders.
  Heads. Faces twisted in anger. Mouths open in a small
  circle of death.
Blood streaming from their severed necks, streaming like
  clouds at sunset.
They came from all directions, screaming my name. Each
  mouth, open in that circle of death, screamed Sweeney,
  Sweeney. On that hill in the middle of that field, they
  circled my head.
A king, one screamed. A northern king, screamed the next.
  The third said, not a king but a madman. The fourth
  said, let us torment the mad king. And the fifth, let us
  chase him into the sea, let us torment him until he
  drowns to escape our words, let us drown him.
Mad? I was not mad. I was Sweeney the king. A king knows
  how to deal with enemies. I lifted my sword.
They flew at me. One bit my knee, another the nape of my
  neck. I struck and struck. They were swifter than
  swords.
There was nothing to do but this: I rose into the air. The
  battle shrank beneath me. I saw men knotted together
  in life and in death. I saw carrion crows gather, drawn
  by the warm smell of blood. I saw, on the side of the
  field, a woman leading away a white cow.

I flew to a high crag, but the heads flew with me. The crash
of a head against my thigh. Against my shoulder.
Against my own head. Blood streamed from them like
water. I was red and wet with blood.

They screamed Sweeney, Sweeney. You saw the light die in
our eyes. Let us have that moment with you, again. The
light dying. Light. Dying. Light. Again.

I did not know them. I had killed so many. All had names
once, and histories. I did not know them. How could
they know me?

I rose again, higher. They said I would drown myself in the
sea. No.

I wrapped myself in clouds. I hid there, brilliant and white
and cold. No one guessed, looking up from Mag Rath,
that the king was there, high in the clouds, singing his
battle song like a new fledged bird.

4. The Ivy-Tops

Dark has fallen. It grows cold. I have had no rest since
meeting my enemy. Aha, they are dead, they are dead,
they could not kill me. I rose above them and kicked
until they rolled away like rotten apples in a dying
orchard. They are dead, dead, they could not kill me.
I tear at crimson silk until I am free and naked in the red
dusk.
Feathers, I say, feathers! My skin prickles in the high wind.
Now I fly, sleek and strong, high above that field. I see
the battle's dainty pattern: retreats, advances, the
ragged lines of war. I sing my victory song.
Men tire me. I want to sit in a crabapple and eat sour fruit. I
want to perch in a twisted oak and feast on acorns.
Trees call out to me, here, stop here, come down here.
They wave their offerings of fruit and seeds. Northwest
I go, into the hills in search of an ivy-topped tree.
In Bearaigh forest I alight, wings weary from flight. I sing
softly, my victory song. But I hear noise: men, armed
men rushing into the wood. I hear them calling.
Sweeney, they say, come down to us. Slender Sweeney,
leader of hosts, comely crystal-eyed king, come down.
Lead us again into battle, red-handed Sweeney, man of
gore. Come back to us now, Sweeney, Sweeney, they
call.
My feathers rise and spread. Sweeney? Do I know that
name? I cannot fit my thin tongue around it. Why do
they call Sweeney, Sweeney? I knew someone of that
name, once, in a place called Mag Rath. I grow curious. I
wish to meet him again.
In my heart lies a map. It shows the way to a four-gapped
glen tumbling with waterfalls, green with cress and
sorrel, black with sloe. Clean banks where I can nest,
great ivy-topped trees where I can perch. I must fly
there. I must not sleep until I find that place without

sword, without spear, without mead, without warriors, without kings.

Glen Bolcan: Sweeney is there. In my heart is the map. The journey is long from roost to roost. I must begin.

5. Rooks at Sunset

Light softens to gold. Violet streaks the west. Night gathers
   like mist, calling to itself all hooded ghosts and
   phantoms on dark wings.
There was a time I heard screams in the dusky sky and
   walked on, never lifting my eyes. There was a time I saw
   dark forms gather in skeleton trees and walked on,
   thinking them only birds come home to roost.
I slept then, and dreamed. Dreamed of falling and falling,
   dreamed of dark wolfish dogs, dreamed of narrow
   passes over high blue hills. I awoke in those pale dawns
   and walked the world of men, daylit and kingly.
I no longer sleep. Sleep is for those who are not yet awake. I
   know the truth of this world now, its dark forces
   searching for carrion. I will not lie down, neck open to
   the sky, and let the birds of dreams peck out my eyes.
I watch as they gather, spiraling down in the dying light. I
   listen as they gather, shrieking tales of dying warriors
   whose intestines they have eaten.
I know a roost by its reek of war. As those ghosts descend, I
   climb.
They alight around me, screaming. I scream out my own
   tales of dying warriors. The sound is like the din of
   battle.
Ghosts cannot find those who hide among them. Slowly the
   gray phantoms grow silent. Darkness blankets me. I too
   grow silent. Naked legs wrapped around the tree's hard
   trunk, I stand watch through the long night.

6. Flights of Praise

Every dawn, I leave my roost and fly east into the pearling
sky.

Before the sun rises I am on Knockaulin, there to greet her
with my little song. As she leaves night's embrace, I
welcome her, sun of the seasons, lady of light, mother
of all.

And then fly southwest, to sweet Slieve Bloom, heart of the
island, mountain of secret springs. There I dance and
twitter, celebrating the warming air and the slant silver
light of morning as the sparrow welcomes me from
thickets of bramble.

And then further west, to dark Slieve Mis, heavy blue
guardian of waters. On her smooth steep sides I swoop
and dive, announcing the stark sun of noon. The duck
and drake welcome me from sleek lakes, and the call of
the wild goose echoes through the hills.

Along the rocky coast and high barren hills I trace the day's
progress. To Slieve Echghte I go with its flanking
valleys, then north to cloud-shadowed Beana Beol with
hidden heather islands on fingers of gray water. There
the gray ghosts of hoodie-crows carve patterns in the
bogland as their harsh call shatters the golding light.

North again, to the sharp sides of Cruachan Aige as the
prophet mountain shimmers in the declining light.
There I sing alone, a small stray bird on a snowy
summit beside a great circle of stone. There I bow and
bow to the sun as she slips blushing into the bright
western waters and into the night's waiting arms.

And then, in the gathering dark, I fly to a small northern
hill where, in silence, I listen to my beating bird's heart
and thank the sun and the earth for its lively rhythm.
There I remember the joys of other lives: spawning as a
frog, dancing as a light-haired maiden, carrying an
immense leaf as an ant, hunting in the hedgerows as a

stoat.

Shadows of old nightmares come then, too, but distant,
distant as Slieve Mis from Emain Macha. I can outfly
them now, as I do each night when I make my solitary
way to Glen Bolcan, sweet refuge of ivy-topped oaks.

7. Dark of the Moon

How she changes, my lady queen, how she changes. When
she was fat and fair-faced, I shed my feathered cloak and
ran naked with wolves beneath her gleaming glance.
How we howled then, how we howled and ran.
But she grows lean and stern of late. Tonight she is a
somber shadow, darkness on darkness. We have grown
silent, we dwellers in cold forests. I crouch against the
hard bark and hear the yew breathe.
I remember heat and song, stone walls hung with fur, the
sweetness of mead. Huge men draping themselves
against pale women. A harper playing slow airs. Dogs
beneath our feet, growling in sleep. Everything dark
with passion and gloom. Everything dark while fire
blazed and candles gleamed on metal.
In this forest, no fire. Only waiting, in cold darkness.
In that time I was a warrior. I fought the darkness. I
demanded light, light, light. I killed for light. I burned a
fat slave alive to illuminate my halls. I pressed oil from a
silkie to light my bronze lamps.
Such light only deepens shadows. I called for more light,
more light.
And the shadows grew and deepened.
Beyond this forest are kings like that. I fear them. They
would plunder the forest for fuel. They would take this
old yew and leave me no home. They would steal my
lady queen to burn in their braziers.
Then darkness would eat me. Cold would devour me. I
would die naked beneath a blackthorn, keening for the
moon.

Snow is falling. In my cloak of feathers, I shiver as ice rimes
my face.

From my forked tree I watch the great stag pass. I have seen
him push his horns against those of other stags, seen
him push antlered heads to the ground. How splendid I
would be, riding between his antlers, answering to Fer
Benn, king of the horned ones.

Next comes the wolf, long shadow on snow, gray against
the glinting ice. I have seen her take a lame doe, heard
her call the pack to its red meal. How splendid I would
be, riding on her, hands twisted in her rough fur,
answering to Fer Fiach, king of the hunters.

And now that unruly animal whose call stills the forest. A
large herd this time, more raucous than crows. The
voice of this beast makes me shiver until the ice in my
feathers tinkles.

I do not want to ride on their brazen backs, for they would
not take me to the mountains of wild Mis or the rocky
peak of Callan, but to a plain near a river that would
soon smell of death. They would call me Sweeney and
take me to Mag Rath.

I am a bird now, cold and hungry and thin. I hold myself
silent and still. I know all bird languages. When the owl
croons, I look up at the floating moon. When the geese
bray, I look for swelling buds. But I do not know this
creature's harsh tongue. It is empty of the sea song and
the breaking dawn and the comfort of clear water.

They gather beneath me, tracing in the snow the shape of a
carrion crow. Their calls grow louder. They point west,
north, east. They push each others' shoulders. Their
faces redden.

The forest is silent. We are watching. We shiver and wait.

9. War among the birds

Loud screams. Harsh calls. Strange music in the dawn.

In half-dream I recognize the sound of battle. I remember it
from long ago, from a fort-ringed field. I have not heard
it since.

I am cold. Under my skin, sleek with feathers, I am hollow.
I could feel my heart once, my blood, my flesh. I was a
warm home with a hot fire. Now I am a dark cave on a
winter night.

The sounds grow louder. I hide my face in my wings. I have
seen enough of heads flying through the air and the
shape of a single hand, still grasping a sword, on the
bright green grass. I have seen enough of arms rising
and falling. Enough of blood, blood, blood, enough.

The sounds grow louder. Strident screaming from my left.
A soft croon to my right. Screaming, screaming,
screaming.

I do not move. I close my eyes. If I see one more battle, my
wits will leave me. I will forget who I am and fly, mad
and raving, from my yew-home.

Screaming. Screaming. Now should come the bronze sound
of weapons. The pounding of feet, the swish of flesh
dividing, the heavy sound of falling bodies. But no. No.

Twittering. Something like a melody. Moans again. The
sounds move, making patterns around my yew-home.
The sounds repeat and repeat and repeat.

In the loudness of battle there was one sound I remember
above all, a soft gurgle as life was released from the
throat of a man. If I could fly from here and not hear
that sound again, I would do so, but that would mean
lifting my wings from my eyes and seeing red again, red
and hacked limbs and twisted faces.

In silent darkness, I await that sound.

It does not come. The sounds repeat, repeat, forming
patterns around my tree. They begin to seem like

melodies. I begin to find them beautiful.

Am I going mad? How can I think war beautiful? Enough of war and your dreams become all screaming heads. Enough of war and you forget all other beauties, the small spring flowers and the yearning bend of willows and the sweet taste of water.

Yet the song of battle has come again to me. We sing it at dawn, we birds, when we define the boundaries of our kingdoms. In repeating glissades, in wild crescendos, in syncopation, in fierce trills, we do our battle with each other.

I lift wings from eyes. My throat opens and I sing. La-la-lee, la-la-loo. La-la-lee, la-la-loo. A simple song, for I am just a small drab bird in a yew tree. Over and over. My heart returns. My blood, my heart, my flesh, all become song. I sing and sing and sing.

10. In the Cold Night

Cold pierces me, hunger pierces me, ceaseless pain pierces
me. I am the wildman of the snow.

Other men judge me as no man: half-bird, half-naked,
feathered, clad in tatters. But I am still Sweeney, still a
man even if a mad one.

Look for me in the trackless places, for I will not set foot
upon your paths. I stay on the move, for that is the way
of my kind.

My hands are striped with red, my cold hands, cut by bare
gray branches. My feet are cold and bare, my cold feet,
their coverings of cloth and flesh torn off by briars.

My hands shake like an old man's. My mind is confused. I
do not know if I am in the southwest, on the dark
looming mountain, or in the far north on a cairn-
crowned peak, or on the gray mountains near the
narrow sea.

I hear something. It is my voice. I am crying out from the
mountain of eagles. I am crying out from the blue
island. From the great gray sea, a moan comes forth: it
is me, a sad mad man.

The night is long and cold. Day will come, no better. I will
pull plants from the side of a well and stuff my mouth
with them. I will eat white flowers.

It is sad that I killed and was not killed. My old enemies,
have no fear: I am weak now, weak and mad and naked
in the cold night.

Last night I slept in the cleft of that ancient yew that rises
   from rock to shake gnarled fists at a low streaming sky.
The other trees on the hill—muscle-bound beech and
   dainty elm—were empty ghosts of winter. Their
   branches no shelter. No shelter from cold rain and wind
   stung with the sea's sharp salt. Only one gray-tufted
   yew, cleft by storm, for a madman's bed.
When the sky turned in its bed and tugged at the cover of
   darkness, I awoke, thirsty for fresh water. My feet found
   rock after rock, a hidden path beneath dank ivy and the
   slime of rotting leaves. I moved, a shadow in shadows,
   toward the sea.
Rock. Rock. Rock. The sky raising itself above me. Rock.
   Rock. The rock graying. The forest graying. Rock. The
   sky graying and pearling and yellowing.
In a cleft in a high rock hill, water hid itself until the red
   sun rose. As light shattered on water, I drank the first
   cold drops of spring.
Beside me, a gorse bush shredded into bloom. At my feet,
   snowdrops opened like winter memories.
The water laughed. I knew you then, well-guardian, fiery
   arrow. I knew you waited to know me.
I am Sweeney the mad. I was once a king, eager to arms, my
   sword singing of the hot blood of young men.
Battle was mead to me then. My sword drank the hot blood
   of young men. Mothers wept when I sang my battle
   song, and I answered with laughter.
Was it you at Mag Rath? Was it you, generous woman of
   the gray laughing eyes? Was it you I saw, leading a
   white cow beside a clear stream?
I remember that stream. I cut a man in half as he stood
   there. The water ran red. I remember his eyes. An

instant of knowing.

Was it you at Mag Rath? Woman who turns back the tides
of war, was it you drove me mad? And now offers sweet
water? Water for mad Sweeney. Sweet water and rock.
Was it you at Mag Rath?

12. The Woman

Snowdrops and watercress and cool well water: this is my feast.

Snowdrops my bread, watercress my meat, water my mead. This is the way a king lives, in the forest. This is the way a mad king lives.

This is my castle, this ivy-topped oak which has room for one mad king who needs no warriors. And the cress-covered well, its bank lined with snowdrops, this is my feasting hall.

A woman has come. I see her, walking on small feet into the forest.

She carries a basket decked with silk ribbons. She sings as she walks on her small feet. She swings the silken basket. She moves towards the well. She leans down to fill her basket with cress.

Oh, woman, are you not someone's daughter? Is he a king? Does he live in an ivy-top and drink from a well? Would you leave him to die, starved and parched in the top of a tree?

I had a daughter. I remember her now. I came home from battle, covered with gore, holding the head of a stranger. The eyes, glazed in death, stared. The hair was stringy with blood. I tossed the head at her feet, laughing.

She did not weep. She never wept. She was a fine proud girl. She bowed to me, silent and stern. She turned and departed. The next day came news: she had leapt to her death from the cliffs near our home.

She was a fine proud girl. A girl like you, though not so merry. If I had her back, I would feed her snowdrops and let her sip cool water from my hands. If I had her back, I would teach her my dawn-song. If I had her back, I would cover her at night with my wings and croon her to sleep.

But she is dead, dead, dead from shame.

Oh, woman, take my little feast. Eat merrily. Sing as you
leave the forest. As for me, I will fly to the west. There
are hard cliffs there, a wall against the sea. Even a bird
can die there, if he is full enough of sorrow to plummet
like a rock to the sea.

Why do your eyes shine, daughter of strangers? How has
the well come into my eyes? What is this softness
against my face?

Name? Have I a name? Oh, daughter, how can I tell you?
You would turn from me, you would take your tender
hand from my cheek, you would not catch my tears with
your tender fingers.

Have you ever heard stories of Sweeney the mad? I am
someone like him. Once a king, now a madman who
sings like a bird. I am someone like him.

What is this? Drink from your hands? Eat this small bunch
of cress?

Oh woman, oh daughter. Such kindness. Such kindness.

I must tell you the truth: I am Sweeney the mad. On the
field at Mag Rath I heard voices, saw visions. All the
dead men came to me, and I flew away like a bird in the
sky. I live in this tree and I eat from this well. I am
Sweeney the mad.

Oh woman, oh daughter. Keep your fine cloak. My wings
are enough. Yes, I grow cold when winter snows come.
Yes, I grow hungry when cresses die back. But this is
my home, this ivy-topped oak.

Here, daughter, a gift from mad Sweeney who has only
feathers. Let this one be yours.

PART FIVE

Here Be Dragons

Once upon a time a map was
a story, a story was a map,
and time and space and
history and place were one.

Then boundaries appeared and
with them, exactitude: maps became
clocks, ways of being more and
more certain of the ends of things.

But the world itself is not a map.
Every instant something changes. No
map can be perfect for long. We
had to solve that problem: now

no river can meander, no tree be cut
unmapped. Now, every instant, we
redraw to increasing perfection
a map with no names or stories,

a purposeful map, a map with no
unknowns nor any hesitancies,
a pinpoint map, an omniscient map
that even maps you there

reading these words, even maps
the hairs on your arms as you read
this: inside the tip of each bomb
we are drawing the perfect map.

Mars in the Northern Sky

I
With Mars invisible in a white sky
and mountains like smoke in the west
I am halted by reddening rosehips
that predict snow before equinox
and recall for me the summer
when late rains swelled the rivers,
the year of the Pacific war.

II
A month later, the rot of flood.
A month later, napalmed children,
flesh hanging like shreds of birch bark
in spring. Just past solstice now,
snow powders the northern domes,
blinding flyers, killing lovers
after rosy mountain weddings.

III
And in mountains far to the east
all the dancers at a wedding
are ripped into red pieces
by bombs dropped by the children
of the bombers of that summer
when arctic rivers flooded and
my brother trained as an assassin.

IV
In a sky the color of the birch
that marks the forest boundary
Mars is invisible but present.
Roses sway, predicting winter,

their rich smell of promise
so beautiful, so threatening.
Far away, bodies bloom red.

Ise Shrine, August 15

A millennium
ago the Yamato queen
established this shrine
for imperial worship.

She had never seen
a white-skinned woman like me,
had no idea that
such an intruder would come.
Even in her dreams
the people were just like her.

She did not take care
to forbid entry to me
and people like me.
Even if she had been told
of our existence,
she would not have believed it.

Of course she could not
imagine Nagasaki,
Hiroshima, Little Boy
and Enola Gay.

The cedars rise like torches
from the heat of rocks.
Fluttering prayers tied to trees
invoke the goddess.
I am the white nightmare here.
I am the ghost of all hate.

Hmong Pa-ndau,
Embroideries of the Laos Hills

A woman buys a dream maze in blue and red
on a patio in California while the sun
rages like a warrior, while the wind battles
with the sea for possession of the sand.
She does not know who cut and stitched
the runes of slavery in the cotton cloth,
what old mother bent beneath the mission tiles
to trace an alphabet of tribal names and to reach
back over the Pacific to the peaks of home.

The woman takes the maze away, back across
the sea in the direction of the Laos hills
and hangs it on the wall above her bed.
She dreams: in a neat small hut, laughing,
away from any wars; in a trackless jungle, fleeing,
short of breath; explosions and escapes. She dreams:

solitudes and sorrows, forgotten families.
She dreams while an old woman who has sold
these dreams for bread sleeps fitfully, trying
to find the road back, trying to remember scenes
that shine like dragons' scales, weeping in her sleep
for the one time she forgot to trap the power
of dreams within a border of embroidered peaks.

The Woman of Baghdad

She rises in the glow of a red sun
to make strong coffee. She fills her
cup with sugar from the bowl
her grandmother used. She sits
drinking slowly, beneath her lime tree.

I can see her through the blue glow
of the news: she moves with deliberate
grace in the silence of her morning.
As she reaches up to pull her hair
back from her neck, I see the tiny age
spots beginning on the back of her hand.

Men are talking somewhere, but she
does not hear them. She hears the murmur
of a dove in the tree. She hears the tiny
roar of a city wakening. She hears her heart
as we all hear ours, a soundless sound.

The men are saying she will die. The men
are saying the bombs are coming.
She, hearing nothing, gets up heavily
and picks a single lime from her tree.
She breathes its oily fragrance. These
are the last breaths she will take.

Geography Lessons

How I learned my world:
born six months after Hiroshima,
learned to speak with names
of Bolovogue and Limerick,
Augrim and Vinegar Hill,
lost battles in a lost land;
learned to read on father's letters
from Japan as he bombed
Pusan, Inchon, Chosin;

celebrated ninth birthday
the day Churchill begged us
not to use A-bombs to defend
Quemoy and Matsu;
celebrated tenth birthday
practicing duck-and-cover
in case the Russians came.

How I learned my world:
battle after battle after battle,
Saigon, Hanoi and Cuba,
My Lai, Khe Sahn,
Pleiku, the Tonkin Gulf.
Now Basra and Tikrit, Kirkuk,
Umm Qasar, Najariah.
Seoul again, and Panmunjon.
Nablas, Ramallah, Hebron.

This is not the way
I want to know my world.

In west Iraq there is a town.
Only one road leads to it.

It is too far from any oil
or water to be important.
I do not know its name.
So far it has been overlooked.
A woman lives there,
a widow my age.
She has dark eyes.
She has a garden.

I know there is a town
like that. I know
there is a woman
like that, in that town.

This is my wish for her:
That she name her own land
and its familiar hills
in words I never know.
That she live and die
safe in its severe beauty.

This is my wish for her:
that I never hear of her.
That she never hears of me.

The Peace Conference Shares Space with the Arms Bazaar

The first day we all had the run
of the hotel, the whole place,

even the beautiful airy downstairs
lobby and the palatial ballroom

on the second floor. It was peaceful;
nuns and men in uniform mingled,

there really was room enough for us all.
But the next day the way to the lobby

was barricaded with tables. We were told
the space had been filled with weapons,

missiles we were forbidden to see.
Then the ballroom was shut off:

something about a secret satellite.
That afternoon parts of the main floor

disappeared behind black bunting.
By the end, every hour was a closure.

If we could not enter the rooms
filled with weapons, we could not

ignore them either. It was not just
space they occupied. They changed

the possible paths we could walk.
By the end we were moving, two

by two, through the only open space,
the narrow route that led outside.

Grief in the Gallery

Every wall
here shows Abel
on his knees
and staring up at Cain
with a resilient disbelief
that there is such a thing as
violence—

we used to tease
you for your innocence
because you said

we make peace with our gaze,
we must look only
at what we wish to thrive,
we must look carefully—

ah friend
to know you died
shaking your head
the reasons why
your murder was insane,
unreasonable,
all your plans
still on your breath
right to the end—

Hiroshima Mon Amour

When we touch each other
we make a treaty, an entreaty,
with our histories: your father
left Poland just in time,
my grandfather left Ireland
just in time, your father
was not exterminated,
my grandfather did not
become an assassin—

Have you ever been marched
down the street in Nevers,
shorn for love? Have you
never? The forlorn lovers

on the screen entreat
each other's trust, beside you
the German woman, beside me
the English man—Hiroshima,
Hi-ro-shi-ma—we know
nothing, nothing at all,
we do not even always
understand the language,
we do not even always
understand, and the Laotian
behind us whispers the meaning:

Have you ever been marched
down the street in Nevers,
shorn for love? Have you
never? Your father would have

spit in the eye of the German
woman, my grandfather would have
refused to sit beside the English
man, that Laotian behind us
is translating a poison tongue,

how much we have reason to hate,
how much reason there is to be guilty,
how much reason there is to hate us

—sitting together in the dark—

when we touch hands
it is an entreaty

The River, Constructed by Saddam Hussein and Named the Mother of Battles, Speaks

I was built in a rage of blame.
I was built in pride and anger.
I was built as a rippling flag.

But I am more than they expected.
I have planted small reeds
along my straight shores,
I have sung sing to waterbirds
who crowd into me, nesting.

I have deepened and settled.

In ten years date palms
have lined my curving banks.
In a hundred years I will have
sloughed out lakes and passages.
In a thousand years I will have birthed
green islands on my blue surface.

And they will have blown away like sand.
They will have faded like morning flowers.
They will have dried up like light rain.

The Tiniest of Prayers

Paper burns easily. It does not take
a bomb to destroy these words, nor

an explosion to drown a voice in a silent
room. It does not take the world's end

for prayers to be unheard. Smaller violence
suffices. But as you read this, ten thousand

poets are raising their pens. A million songs
are being chanted into the precious air.

When all we have's so temporal, so fragile,
small prayers must suffice. We pray on paper

that the world does not yet end:
we act in concert to sustain it.

Red-Tailed Hawk

Just past dawn in early fall,
a sparrow screamed at me
as I walked into the woods.

I did not grasp the warning.

Beside the dry creekbed,
I stopped at the shore
of a dark pool of silence.

At its center, a hawk.

Five feet away, chevrons
and arrows on his chest,
talons and beak like knives.

He stared at me. I stared at him.

At that moment, to the east,
men were debating ways to kill.
In the forest, deadly beauty.

I had never seen a hawk so close.

He looked left and right, his beak
a cruel and graceful curve.
His chest heaved in a breath, a sigh.

He flew straight at me.

I could not move. His wings
were as wide as I am tall.
I simply stood and waited.

He veered away,

alighted in a nearby tree.
Wonder filled me, rushing in
like water down a dry streambed.

Hawk, I whispered, hawk,

and stared straight at him,
into his hard eyes.
Hawk, my heart sang, hawk,

a word of death and life

in balance, a word of death
and hunger and fierce pain
and beauty and devouring.

I spoke the name of one

who wastes no life, who knows no
anger, whose strength is pure, whose
only weapon is his feathered self.

Hawk, I whispered, hawk.

Winner of a 2004 Pushcart Prize for literature, Patricia Monaghan is the author of three previous collections of poetry. *Seasons of the Witch,* a cycle of poems connecting the passages of a woman's life with the seasons, won a 1994 Friends of Literature prize for the best book of poetry by a Chicago author. Its second edition, with a CD of poems set to music by several composers, won the 2003 Best Multi-Media award from COVR, the Coaltion of Visionary Retailers. She has also written several encyclopediae of mythology including the recent *Encyclopedia of Celtic Myth and Folklore* (Facts on File, 2004). Her nonfiction work includes *The Red-Haired Girl from the Bog: The Landscape of Celtic Myth and Spirit* (New World Library, 2002). She teaches science, literature, and mythology at DePaul University in Chicago. Poems from *Homefront* have been set to music by folk composer Michael Smith and performed by vocalist Jamie O'Reilly on the CD, *Songs of the Kerry Madwoman.*

Printed in the United States
61364LVS00006B/31-81

9 781933 456096